Like a Second Layer of Skin

Like a Second Layer of Skin

100 Affirmations for Faithful Living

Dorothy Winbush Riley

RESOURCE *Publications* • Eugene, Oregon

Resource Publications
A division of Wipf and Stock Publishers
199 W 8th Ave, Suite 3
Eugene, OR 97401

Like a Second Layer of Skin
100 Affirmations for Faithful Living
By Riley, Dorothy Winbush
Copyright©2001 Pilgrim Press
ISBN 13: 978-1-60608-804-3
Publication date 5/14/2009
Previously published by Pilgrim Press, 2001

This limited edition licensed by special permission of The Pilgrim Press.

Contents

Preface	vii
Writing Affirmations	x
I Am the Sower	1
Love Is of God	11
I Hold the Seeds	25
The Image I Show	37
I Am Renewed by the Power of My Mind	47
I Master My Thoughts	57
I Am Awesomely and Wonderfully Made	69
I Forgive and I Am Forgiven	77
I Open Myself to the Circle of Prosperity	87
I Speak Words that Are Sweet to the Soul and Healing	97

Preface

My mother warned me to be careful of the words I spoke because they created my world. Nevertheless, I had to learn it for myself, and I learned through joyful and painful experiences that each person is born with the power of creation at the tip of the tongue. My affirming words came true with my first job as an information operator, when I heard and fell in love with the name Schiavi. I visualized a beautiful baby girl, proclaiming that I would have a baby girl and her name would be Schiavi. I spoke about Schiavi as if she was with me because Schiavi was real to me. And just as the Prophet Isaiah said, "Then suddenly I took action, and all my predictions came true." My words were prophetic; today Schiavi is the proud mother of my first grandchild, Nandi.

Affirmations are simple statements of truths that provide positive control over random destructive thoughts. *Like a Second Layer of Skin* is a book of affirmations that transformed my negative thoughts and self-talk. As a child, I talked at a supersonic rate and stuttered badly. Consequently, I didn't talk much and became a quiet bookworm. Twenty years later, at Wayne State University, my supervising teacher suggested I go to a speech therapist for teacher endorsement. The lessons I learned provided power to control my speech by planting suggestions and controlling the flow to my mind. Despite that experience, it was years before I truly believed that I was the author of my reality and that I lived the dramas created by my imagination, my thoughts, and my words.

Affirmations are more than just speaking or giving lip service; they show how and what you think, feel, and believe about yourself. They helped me control my roller coaster dieting. No matter how many diets I tried, nothing worked until I changed my feelings and fears about weight, stopped fearing fat, and focused on a healthy body. I discovered my overweight condition was the result of wrong thinking that led to wrong eating habits and other unhealthy behaviors. My words established a belief system that led directly to the heart of all problems. I learned that to escape an unhappy condition, the cause must be changed, not the symptoms. Once I decided I wanted to be healthy, I no longer worried about being fat. When you find happiness; you no longer try to escape unhappiness. When you have the recipe for success; you no longer worry about failure. As you live each day of your life, you discover who you are and what you are, then you affirm with faith your identity and purpose; you are empowered to change your world.

As situations occurred in my life, I learned that the words I speak and visualize vibrate with energy, becoming the creative or destructive laws of my life. The thoughts I believed and affirmed about my health, my work, my family, and my success became real. Even the words I said jokingly came true. I live life through my words and to receive blessings, I had to imagine, speak and feel blessings. I had to align my words with my actions. I could not hide an envious heart or divided tongue with the wings of an angel. They did not fit. I had to transform my mind.

Before I think or speak, an idea springs from somewhere beyond limitations. Ideas have power and come from the divine presence of the Creator. As the idea blossoms, it guides and directs my thinking as I become a lightning rod of energy using each creative idea as a spark from the mind of God.

If you are not living up to your divine potential, and you are not all that you are supposed to be, take time to inventory your mind and see whether your thoughts and words are confused, causing reverse thinking and reverse actions in your life.

After you clarify your consciousness, understand who you are and whose you are, and you will realize that you are truly a special person. Think of yourself in a new way, and you will freely speak of yourself without the strait-jacketed stranglehold of the opinions and beliefs of others. Howard Thurman said, "How much of [our] destiny turns on the magic of words! . . . Words, words, words, the mark of [humanity's] freedom."

We are always believing something about ourselves and are, therefore, planting thought seeds in our subconscious soil. Those thought seeds grow according to the programming within the seed. Fruit grows from fruit seeds and vegetables seeds yield vegetables. Weeds come from weed seeds just as a rose comes from a rose. This is true for the seeds we plant and affirm in our minds. Negative thinking on sickness, loneliness, poverty, and pain, if nurtured and allowed to grow, become real experiences.

Affirmations are spiritual words of excellence from a high level of thought. They require tender loving care and special attention to your thoughts, actions, and words to maintain that excellence. Affirmations let us know that we are connected to an Infinite Power that is always ready to flow through our lives. After we make the decision to affirm and open unlimited possibilities, the laws of love, prosperity, health, and all other spiritual laws take effect. Your affirmations are road maps to a creative energy field and a faith-filled life.

You will affirm as I have in this affirmation: "I have the ability to use my thoughts and words; the ability to direct what I say and how I say it; the ability to neutralize the past; the ability to recreate myself; the ability to change my belief structure and flow freely with life. I have the ability to train my thinking by selectively speaking words that release old patterns, old pains, and old perceptions. I have the ability to change my world by changing the words I speak about my feelings, attitudes, and expectations."

Writing Affirmations

Whatever you desire when you pray, believe that you have it, and you will have it. Jesus also said that when you pray, if you expect to receive a positive response, forgive and release negativity from your mind. If your affirmations are to be successful, you must believe you can change your mental state to get certain results in your body, affairs, and relationships. Once you affirm, you leave the blurred past and begin to live in today's light; you release old hurts, self-defeating anger, and the crippling fears that sabotage your happiness, success, and health. In speaking and writing your affirmations, clear your mind of confusion and put your desires on paper.

Write affirmations for yourself using the first person singular. I am. I can. Include self-imagery and meditate daily.

Make your affirmations fit you *Like a Second Layer of Skin* by finding your resonance, vibration, or frequency. You might write your affirmations to a favorite piece of music that connects and resonates with your vibrations.

Write your affirmations in present time. You can't change the past and the future is unpredictable. Deal with the present.

Be honest with yourself. Write affirmations truthfully, briefly, simply, and clearly. Speak the words until they are embedded in your mind.

Affirm what you desire, not what you do not want.

Think about what you clearly desire and why it is right for you.

Write your affirmations with emotionally–and positively–charged words. Imagine what it feels like to be happy, healthy, loved, successful, and confident. What does that sound like? What does it feel like? How and what is the smell and taste?

Find your life's purpose by deciding what you want to do with your life. It is yours and your responsibility to live it with passion.

Define your goals. What is your short-term goal? Do you have a long-term goal? Do you know your talents and abilities to help you live fully and faithfully?

I Am the Sower
I sow the words that
vibrate with faith,
power and truth.

1

1 Power

I
and only I
have the power to make me
happy or unhappy.
I
and only I
have the power to make me
loving or unloving.
I
and only I
have the power to make me
rich or poor.
I
and only I
make of
My life what it is
to be.

2
Power Words

My words are powerful.
I listen and I speak words filled with love and
compassion knowing the creative impact they have on
my life and those around me.

I declare with ever-increasing belief that
the Spirit within me can control my tongue
as I take responsibility for my words.
I speak words inspired by truth
and when I take action all my predictions
come true.

3
Prayer

I pray
because prayers change things.

My prayers are life-changing and life-creating.

I pray so the Creator
can change me and show me what He
desires for my life.

When I pray, I become more human as I offer
loving hope to each person I meet.

I know the universe is orderly,
but when I pray in the right way
I can change
the path of the world.

4
Mood for Prayer

I bring my mood
to thoughts of God and I practice **praying**.

I fill my mind with love.
I stop trying to solve problems.
I empty my heart of fear and **worry**.

I pray to become the kind of **person who can**
work for truth.
I pray for others as I seek blessings **for myself.**

I have the power to dream;
my prayers are those visions **waiting to**
become real.

Words

I no longer speak words that are wasted in the wind.

I speak words of
why woman wondering
waking words.
Wisdom womb wonderful
warming words.
Write worldly worthwhile
worshiping words.
Witty wizardly wistful
wishing words.
Watchful wealth working
weaving words.

I speak womanist words.

6
Today

I have everything I need within myself.
I live today and I do something new.
I believe
I state
I announce
I declare
I affirm
I accept
I know
It has already happened.

Healthy Words

I speak words that
I want to be true.
This is my body, and it is the only body that I have.
It is the only body I can have and will ever have.
I am strong. I am energetic. I am enthusiastic. I am success.
I am love.

I am a clear thinker with power to receive whatever
I desire.
I am never out of energy or enthusiasm for life.
My body is alive with promise and joy.

Good health is mine.
Every cell grows with health, normally and naturally.
My spirit is healed.
My heart is healed.
My life is healed.

I rest in the certainty of well being.
I relax and allow the One Source
to strengthen
and perfect my mind,
my words,
my body.

8

I Release the Past

I no longer allow belief in past failures or
disappointments to control and determine my existence.

I release blurred vision and confusion.
I release all habitual patterns of resistance
to the forward movement of life.

I am free,
consciously and subconsciously.
I am free with the truth of God.

I accept the truth that good overcomes evil.
I am infused with eternity as I realize the truth
never contradicts itself.

I have the right objectives and goals to
bring every good thing into my life.
I accept the Divine Presence in everything.
I am ready for greatness.

9

Connecting Words

The power that made the red, red rose;
The power that holds the sun, moon,
and stars in the heavens;
The power that makes the rivers flow
and the mountains rise;
The power that makes the seasons change;
This same invisible, infinite power operates in my life
as I connect my mind and word to the power of God.

10

I Progress

I maintain my freedom of choice. I am never
tempted to exchange it for false security.
I am a victor.

I progress over
narrow thinking
illusional television
newspapers or
political promises.

Love Is of God
I love and I am born of God, and know God.

11

Law of Love

The perfect law of love
brings everything
good into my life.

I am love
that creates Love.

I rejoice in freedom and
release all selfishness and
separateness
through the healing
power of love.

12
Lamp of Love

I am a lamp of divine love
radiating light to all I meet.

I look into the mirror of my soul and
marvel as it reflects a
splendid, blazing, infinite light;
a divine love echo spiraling from me into
the lives of others.

I readily allow the energy of love to flow
into everything I do and say.

My love is secure, serene, and sincere.
I love
passionately, persistently, powerfully

with faith

knowing I am surrounded by love.

13

Another Planet, Another Space

Love, I have been with you before;
another time, another place,
another planet, another space.

Don't ask me how, but I know
the texture of your face,
the taste of your lips,
the feel of your hands,
the thoughts in your mind.

I have loved you day and night,
night and day,
enduring every challenge and test.
Time after time
I sought your soul to
complete my search
beyond the light.

Love, I have been with you before;
another time, another place
another planet, another space.

14

I Love

At this time, in this place,
my heart is filled with joy.
No matter where I am,
I am never alone because I love.
Love attracts love
and makes my way perfect.

My love multiplies and I give it freely;
my loves forgives
my love endures
my love lives
my love serves.

The love of God shines upon my spirit.
I bask in the colors of my world.
I am complete.
I am content.
I am loved.

15

I Take Responsibility

I take responsibility
for my conscious choices and my behavior
in relationships that bring
negatives or positives into my life.

What I am comes out when I am with people.
Believing that God is at the center of everything,
I try to hide my secret self.
Yet, my eyes, my tongue, my total body
reveals what is truly in my heart.

I must control the petty
jealousies filled with cutting words that
slip like oil from my tongue.

I want to mean something to others and to the Creator.
I want to do things that can make a difference.
I transform what is on my mind
by showing God's grace to all people;
by walking in the light that casts out shadows;
by spreading love that casts out fear.

16

Great Expectations

I have
great expectations.

I expect others to do well and I encourage them in
their quest for success.

I express my feelings.
I respect myself and
I expect others to respect me.
I love myself and I extend this love.

17

Unconditional Love

Unconditional Love.
I can give unconditional love
when I love myself healthfully.

Today, I practice loving myself.
I buy myself flowers and
send a love note to me.

I wrap myself in silk and satin that
caresses and massages my skin.

I look in the mirror and
speak kind, encouraging words to me.

I light candles and incense then
drink wine to me.

I laugh at myself when I mis-take something.
I love myself as a divine child of the Creator.

18
Oh, My Love

Oh, my love!
I have been a part of you
Since the world began.
I dream of you as a vibrating shape of light
Shouting my name!
Seeking my face.

Oh, my love!
Hold me tightly
as we create rhythm in the
synchronized dance of love.

Oh, my love!
I am here in this space for you.
Let us be together in bliss
as we explore the garden.

Love 2

love wraps itself around me like a second layer of skin.
love guides me through the turbulence of discovering myself.
Love exposes my Light-stripping illusion from my mind.
Love leads me to the sunshine and the Spirit of God.

I am free
I am content
I am whole.

The Light of Love

The light of love melted the ice cap covering my heart
as I escaped the cage of ego, releasing a lonely chain
of despair filled with nameless fears
shadowing my valleys and my mountains.
By grace, I reached level ground to find the
Divine Promise still waiting for me to claim.
The promise of the Creator is mine
no matter where I live, what I do, or what I believe.
The promise of the Creator is mine to receive,
but first I must believe.
First, I must believe.
I must believe.

I am tempted like Lot's wife to look back remembering
sensual pleasures and lustful desires addicting my soul
and destroying my spirit.
At this time in my life I struggle to erase the
beckoning memories from my mind.
I fight to keep the seven demons away proclaiming their
shadows no longer have power over me.
Each step I take to live right and be right is a victory
I celebrate because I have come this far.
I celebrate myself, my sexuality, my creativity, my spirituality, and
my light of love, forgetting those things which are behind and
reaching for those things which are before, I press on . . .

I know the battle is not over.
It is not easy, but I can find a way to stay above the chaos of the world where the enticing lights and sounds bombard my mind.
I will stay on the path leading away
from an artificial life of doubt, pain, and regret.
I fight to stay on level ground every day.
I select the words I speak carefully.
I filter the thoughts that enter my mind, my heart, and my soul.

I have always known the Truth that
I am light itself, reflected in the hearts of everyone.
I am the image of the Divine and my work reflects Him.
I have always known the Truth that
I am every light that shines,
Every ray that brightens the world.
I am the light of love melting the ice cap covering your heart.

21
My Heart Is Open to Love

My heart is open to love.
I'm never alone;
my eyes attract love.

The love of God streams
through me and returns a hundredfold to me.

I am in harmony with love.
I speak words of love.
I dance to the music of love.

I Hold the Seeds...
in my hands and what I decide
to do with them, eat them or
plant them, determines whether
or not I have a harvest.

I Am a Point of Light

I am a conscious point of light,
created in the image and
likeness of God.
I have the power of His word and
I claim the power that is mine.

I claim God as the only presence and power in my life.
I claim abundance and want for nothing.
I claim God as my Father who protects and sustains me.
I claim knowledge and everything I need to know comes to me.
I claim wisdom to act knowing peace comes from the Creator God that is in me.

23

My World Is Made New

Every morning is a fresh beginning and
my world is made new.

I have lived all the days of my life
to reach this day,
this moment.
My spirit is young as creativity flows from
my dreams.

I strive to build, create,
grow and love.

Today is a good day,
and I shall make it a day of blessings.
I shall make a heaven on earth.

Action 1

My body is a temple of God.
I am co-builder of my life.
I have free will to eliminate
all thinking that hinders my growth.
I am as I think I am.

I look into a mirror
and see the truth of the universe
revealed in me.

As day follows night with the sun,
I rise to
greet everyone with
acceptance, love, and faith.

The Maker of the Heavens is in me, as well as in other people.
He is an active part of my life and blesses me as my presence blesses others.

Action 3

I rest,
I relax,
I release.

I recognize that God is
all-knowing,
all-seeing, and
ever-present.

I remember that I am a
Child of the Magnificent one and I can
reawaken the Creative Power that is
my gift to share.

I realize my desires are fulfilled
as I have faith and
I rest,
I relax,
I release.

26

I Hold On

No-thing happens overnight!
Every overnight sensation took time, practice, and patience.

I am responsible for choosing what I do with my life.
I hold on to my dreams; I achieve my goals.
I start today from where I am even if it takes 5,000
nights for them to become real.

27

Choices

The tides rise, the tides fall.
Nature is a cycle and everything happens in its time.

I grow each day.
I direct my mind and I control my emotions.
I make choices that bring joy and happiness at the right time.
I don't sit idly wishing to be somewhere else or someone else.
I act and master the present conditions in my life.
I do not miss anything for if it is mine,
it shall return as surely as Spring.

28

Re-Action

When the best made plans vanish like ice cream in July,
or are changed with the lightning speed of a tornado,
I take a step back, breathe,
regroup, and
    think
before I act.
I react to circumstances calmly,
and faithfully.
I look within for solutions to
challenging problems
I take a step back, breathe,
regroup, and
    think
before I act.
I discover inner talents and strength to provide
answers I had not imagined.
I take a step back, breathe,
regroup, and
    think
before I act.
I accept challenges as opportunities for consciousness-expansion
and self-awareness,
I take a step back, breathe,
regroup, and
    think
before I act.

I Have a Mission

Whatever happens or
does not happen in my life is
right for me and motivates me
to grow.

I have a mission in life.
I have the power to choose, and the
choices I make today
determine the direction I travel.

The Realm of God is within me.
I make my mark by
being true to
my purpose.

30

I Claim

I claim whatever I desire
with faith.

I claim peace.
I claim success.
I claim love.
I claim happiness.
I claim health.

I believe in myself and
I claim freedom to
choose the path I will follow.

31

I Align My Behavior

I align
my behavior with
my words and my conscious desires.

My faith is without limit.
My imagination is endless.
My reasoning powers are infinite.
My love is never-ending.

I no longer contradict myself by saying one thing and
believing another, or saying one thing and
doing another.
I work so that all parts of me are
consistent physically,
mentally, and spiritually.
I act as a limitless divine expression of God.

32

I Am in Unity

I am in
unity with the Universal Mind of God.

I call on it for guidance
when my eyes and ears are bombarded
with illusions of limitation, lack, and evil.

I turn my thinking to the love
and abundance of God.

When my situation seems unbearable,
I rely upon the Word of God to guide me.

I know that whatever and wherever I find myself,
it is my doing.

I create the experiences.
I direct my thoughts
to good, to truth,
and the beautiful.

The Image I Show ...
   to the world reflects how
   I feel about myself.
   I am descended from
   the King of Kings;
   I am special.
   I am royalty.

Image 1

I present the best me
even though I display many faces.

Throughout the day I strive to
remove the chains from my mind.

At any given moment, my profound, wise nurturer emerges
only to be overshadowed by my destructive, silly self
who transforms into a demanding self-centered diva.

I coordinate my many selves so that none
is too extreme or unbalanced.
I express my feelings, and I listen to my body.

Each aspect of me is unique and vital.
I present one face, a collage of my best.

Image 2

I am woman soft and fluid,
Flowing with energy and life-giving seeds.

I am woman soft and yielding,
Weighed with strength that does not diminish with time.

I am woman soft and supple,
Bending with the winds while soaring beyond the clouds.

35

Self-Love Self

I never understood people who said
"YOU can only love another as much as
you love yourself."

I thought it was self-centered, egomania
to love and pay attention to myself. Then
I discovered I didn't truly know me and feared loving myself.
I decided to take an honest look at my good qualities,
my faults, my feelings, including guilt, pain, and anxiety.

It took a while for me to have a relationship with myself.
> To know who I am and where I am going.
> To feel my own pulse and taste my sweat.
> To use my power to choose, decide, and act.

I am not perfect.
I am who I am, and
I love myself even when I make mis-steps;
I accept me.

> It is time for me to pay attention to my desires and
> live my dreams.

It is time to accept change and growth.
It is time to give myself permission to enjoy being me.
It is time. It is time.

36

Best Face

It is important to maintain my car.
It is necessary to paint my house and keep it
sparkling like an emerald.

It is okay to keep myself beautiful.
I am unique. I am special. I am me.

I put my best face forward to travel
the pathway to eternal consciousness.

37

Image 3

My personality shows
who I truly am.
No matter where I find myself,
my personality displays love, warmth, and
understanding.

My personality is a magnet that pulls people to
my courtesy,
kindness,
honesty, and
confidence.

38

I Am Original

I cannot be Xeroxed.
I am not a carbon-copy look-alike of
every other person on the planet.

The combination of all parts of me;
my body
my dreams
my mind
my sensitivity
my sexuality
my spirituality
my talents
my tastes
my words

The Divine Artist created me
like no other.
I am original.

I Look Within

I look within myself and
spend time with myself so
I can know myself.

I began to understand the patterns of my life;
the rhythm of my relationships.
I pursued those things that were easily caught
and gave myself to what was less than divine.
I lived on the edge, always sabotaging myself with
the insecurity of excitement
the adrenaline rush of passion
the uncertainty of promises.

I learn to forgive myself, the more I look within
and accept the excitement of order
the pleasure of peace
the passion of faith
the promise of hope.

40

The Power to Be Me

I claim
the power to be me.

I stop comparing myself to others and
seek my best self through
developing my full potential.

I remove the mask that blocks my
talents and creative expressions.

I accept people as they are.
I see the good in others, and it
is reflected in me.

It is my choice and responsibility to
express who I am without fear or disapproval.

I am God's special handiwork, and I exist for God
In His universe.

41

I Am Unique

I am different from all other people.
I am a unique expression of God.
I access the universal mind to create the
best in life.
I meet my problems with courage and use
them as ways to improve my life.
I use my sense of humor and laugh at myself, especially
when I am tense, angry, and frustrated.
I learn.
I never stop learning, therefore I
grow wiser each passing day.

42
I Am True to Myself

I am true to myself
so that I can be true to others.

I do not allow the temptations of
flattery, criticism, or hatred to
sway me from the values
that are important.

I search within myself
to be sure my words and
actions are uplifting and constructive.

I do what I know in my heart
is right even though I may
stand alone.

43
I Smile

I smile.

I beam a friendly smile
reflecting my inner peace and happiness.
My eyes sparkle with joy
at the beauty of the flowers, the sky, and the
people I meet.

I smile at life.
I smile at the infinite
greatness of God and
accept His blessings with a smile

*I am Renewed by the Spirit of My Mind.
I am alive with faith.*

44

Let It Flow

I am truly
alive with my faith.
I realize that every day is designed for good.

I am happy when things go well and
my faith keeps me stable when things go wrong

I know that in the end all things work for good.
And what I consider good or bad
depends on my point of view.

45

I Connect

I connect with the genius in others as
I surround myself with people who keep
my mind stimulated,
my body healthy, and
my spirit right.

I connect with love that strengthens
my body and renews my spirit.
I surround myself with people I
love and who love me.

46
Like Attracts Like

I attract people into my life
who reflect me.

My attitude is positive and
I surround myself with positive people.
I use my creativity and
imagination to build.

I speak the truth with understanding,
love and
      compassion.

I live my faith and believe
that everything happens for a reason
as I make the choices
that attracts good in my life.

47
Breathe-In

I breathe in love.
    I breathe in hope.
    I breathe in peace.
    I breathe in health.
    I breathe in life.

Faith

Divine love
and divine intelligence surrounds me
in everything I do.

When I look at the sky, the sun and the moon;
when I walk through a field of flowers or cross a river or a lake;
when I breathe oxygen from the flowers and grasses of the field;
I know that the Highest Power who made all of these things
also made me.

I am calm, cool, and confident
knowing the power and wonder of the universe
is available to me despite the conditions of my mind
or my self-imposed responsibilities.

I accept the mind of the
Creator that is in me,
around me, and serves me.
As I believe, it will be.

49

I Help Myself

I cooperate with Life as I realize
I can help myself.

I attract good people into my life.
My appearance is clean, healthy, and radiant.
My attitude is positive, and my body shows it.
I watch my thoughts for they become words.
I direct my faith, love, and thoughts to
healthy channels.
I have the power to choose and decide.

My desires are clean, clear, and convincing.
What I want for myself is right for me,
just as it is right for others.

I resist temptation.
I lead no one into temptation.

I believe in myself.
I share my knowledge and learn willingly from others.
I talk with a pleasant, confident voice.
I walk with confidence, and
I love with confidence,
knowing that everything works together for my good,
good returns to me.

50

By My Fruit

The fruit of my womb
is wonderfully magnificent
like no other
fruit in the universe.
It is divinely ordered and a
blessing to the world.

The fruit of my womb
is powerful as an eagle, yet gentle as a lamb
that goes forth into the world
with the promise of God
to serve, prosper, and love.

51

As I Sow, I Reap

I am content
with who I am and
what I accomplish with my life.

The seeds I plant today
flower into achievements as
I journey to the next level of awareness.

I take time to enjoy this day as I continue to
plant seeds.

There is a law that brings everything
into my life according to my thoughts, choices, and
actions.

I must start from where I am and I will
stay in this place until my
mind is ready for the next level.

Peace

Nothing is
As precious as peace.
Peace of spirit
Peace of mind
Peace of heart
Peace of body
I allow the light of love
to draw peace into my life.

The universe demonstrates
the peace of God in the Heavens.
I fill my heart with this perfect peace
and act in such a way that
I spread peace wherever I am.

53

I Am in Harmony

I am in harmony with God.
I am in tune with the beat of life.
I am never too early or too late.
I am in time.
I am tuned to the rhythm of God.
I fine-tune my life to be like Him.
I am the rhapsody of faith.
I am a melody of peace.
I am a crescendo of love.

I Master My Thoughts
and I think on the things
that are true,
that are honest,
that are just,
that are pure,
that are lovely,
that are of good report.

54

My Mind

My mind weaves a tapestry of loving service.
It is the creative force that fuels my purpose.

My mind plants seeds that spread:
the joy of imagination
the happiness of choice
the goodness of life
the love of learning
the faith of eternity
the strength of purpose
the peace of truth
the beauty of nature
the responsibility of decision
the attraction of attitude
the grace of forgiveness
the power of the word

55

I Trust

I trust my still small voice
directly connected to the Spirit of God.

All problems have answers and the Creator God has
the answers that come when I need them.

I do not struggle or worry about anything.
I release obstacles, and
I accept only good, believing whatever
I need is supplied
to me.

56

I Am Safe

I am safe and secure when I travel.
Divine protection and
Divine love surrounds me wherever I go.

No matter who I meet,
I am surrounded by the protective presence of God
who shields all hurts, harms, and dangers from me.

I turn my fears over to God;
I turn my worries over to God.

I believe God is guiding my feet on
the path of peace, safety, and security.

I ask that I return home safely each
day, and it is given to me.

57
I Choose

I am the center of my universe and
I create my world by the mental pictures
I hold each day.
I have the power to create all that
I choose and accept because I
attract whatever I radiate.
I choose to radiate health.
I choose to radiate peace.
I choose to radiate wealth.
I choose to radiate success.
I choose to radiate happiness.
I choose to radiate love.

58
I Control

I control my mind and the
emotions streaming from it.
Divine guidance leads me to
the right place at the right time,
speaking the right word and doing the
right thing in the right way.

I use reason instead of rage.
I spread joy instead of sorrow.
I exude faith and not fear.
I share love and not hatred.

I Relax

I relax my conscious mind
and release all negatives, envy, and vanity.
I release the poisons of guilt, regret, resentment,
pain, and hatred.

I expect cooperation and help from my loved ones and fellow workers
I dwell in peace and harmony that surrounds me.
I accept mis-steps and mis-takes as learning steps toward
truth.
I realize that I am the truth and the life
as I transcend my mind and realize that
I am to God as
a cloud is to the sky.

I Control My Mind

I control
the thoughts
flowing to and from my mind.

I listen to happy, soothing music
I think of the best things on my job
I remember the best song I have heard
I recall the best people in my life.

My mind manifests all my
needs and desires.

I act as though I am and I will be.
I act as though I have and I will have.
I act as though I believe and it is so.

61

I Change My Inner Thinking

I change my inner thinking
to change my life.

I build a clear picture of my magnificent self.
I set goals that lead to positive growth and change.
I make plans for my life, and, if they don't work, I try again.
With knowledge comes wisdom that
allows me to stop struggling and
find my true place.

62

My Conscious Mind

My conscious mind believes in my imagination.
My conscious mind believes in the impossible.
My conscious mind believes in my actions.
My conscious mind believes in my success.

My conscious mind believes I am special.
My conscious mind believes I make a difference.
My conscious mind believes in the value of my goals.
My conscious mind believes in my success.

My conscious mind believes I deserve recognition.
My conscious mind believes I grow with information.
My conscious mind believes I triumph over negative chains.
My conscious mind believes in my success.

My conscious mind believes I surmount any hurdle.
My conscious mind believes I create opportunities.
My conscious mind believes I attain my goals.
My conscious mind believes I am successful.

63

One Power

I recognize my oneness
with all things and
concentrate on bringing harmony
wherever I find myself.
I open my mind and
my heart to the
divine presence of harmony.

My world is created according
to my thoughts,
therefore, I think and meditate
on order, peace, and harmony.

I praise my friends,
I bless my family,
I enjoy my work,
as I realize we are searching for the
same answers.

I recognize my oneness
with everyone around me and
help them meet their goals.

64

In My Head

There are no monsters under my bed,
they live with me inside my head.
If I travel to a distant place
my monsters are right behind my face.
They never give me any peace;
they have a hold they won't release.

If I am to be truly free
I bless my monsters and let them be.
I transform my very soul
closing up the aching hole.
I go deep, deep inside my mind
accepting the cosmic power I find.
I rename my monsters into angels of light
who watch me through the day and night.

Now there are angels over my bed,
they live with me in my heart and head.
My angels protect me in times of stress,
telling me to release, relax, and rest.
My angels tell me I am beautiful, good, and whole
created from One Power, One Love and One Soul.

I am Awesomely and Wonderfully Made

I Celebrate Each Day

I celebrate
each day of my life.
I honor my age.

I thank God for each year that I live.
I welcome the experiences that have brought me to
this point in my life.

I give the best in all situations and
the best returns to me.

Each day my faith is stronger
as I grow
lovingly,
completely,
and happily.

66
I Celebrate Myself

I celebrate myself.
I celebrate my uniqueness
as I realize I am different
from all other people on this Earth.

I look different and
I am beautiful.

My thoughts are different and
I express them when it is necessary.

My talents are different, and I value each gift the
Lord of Life has given me.

My destiny is different and
I have the responsibility to fulfill it.

I am important.
I have imagination.
I have faith and ability
to do what
I must do and
what I should do.
And so it is!

67

Change Is Safe

I change my point of view.
I am flexible in the midst of change.

Change is safe.
I see life
with innocent eyes where problems are
opportunities to grow,
hurdles to transcend,
mis-takes to re-take;
a natural part of growth.

I see with accepting eyes as
I discover that only
I can affirm myself;
only I can negate myself.

68
Growth

Life is a process of growth and
change that does not stop at this moment.
I have courage in the face of any challenge.
I am confident of my ability to deal with adversity.

I grow with the flow
despite real or imagined problems.

69
Change Flows

Change flows in my life as smoothly
as the moon changes phases,
reflecting the balance,
beauty, and abundance of life.

I accept change.
I embrace change
knowing that it brings growth.

I am part of an ever changing creative
universe that leads to
fresh beginnings, new starts
in an amazing adventure
of eternal fulfillment.

70

I Accept Myself

I break down the
barriers I have built around myself.

I tear down the walls of
excuses that prevent me from living
life dynamically and joyfully.

I stamp out the fire of fear that
Prevents me from doing the best I can.

I stop running from life and
stand still long enough for the Benevolent One to
work through me and with me.

I no longer try to be someone I am not.
I accept myself.

71

My Days

I will not waste
my days
in useless anger
over yesterday's distress
or borrow
beckoning promises
of tomorrow.
I will
be and do
today.

72

I Claim a Healthy Body

I claim
a healthy body that is
my right and my responsibility.

With every breath I breathe, I feel health
streaming through my body.
With every glass of water I drink, my organs
are recharged with radiant health and energy.
With every bite of food I eat, my tissues are
teeming with vital health.

The Divine Spirit of Health directs and guides
me to rebuild every part of my body that needs it.
I direct my mind to
maintain a healthy body.

73

I Love Myself

I love myself.
I approve of me.
I am good to me.

I accept my beginnings, my family, and the seeds of my life.
I am as kind to myself as I am to someone else.

I accept compliments and praise because I am worthy.
I grow and I love the way I continue to learn and expand my mind.

I listen to my body, my heart, and my inner self.
I love with passion and strength.
I recognize God in me and I
approve of myself.
I love myself.

I *Forgive and I am Forgiven.*

74

I Forgive Myself

I forgive myself.
I forgive each hurt that has
happened in my life
as I forgive the person I feel
caused the pain.

I forgive each act of
hatred, envy, selfishness, and fear.

I forgive all mistreatment and discouragement
as I forgive my mis-steps and mis-takes.

I forgive and I forget.
I value my mis-takes as precious
treasures of self discovery,
lining a pathway to wisdom, health,
prosperity, and love.

75

I Freely Forgive

I fully and freely forgive.

God's peace removes my fears and strengthens my faith.
His wisdom teaches me;
His hands protect me;
His grace sustains me;
His word feeds me;
His presence surrounds me;
His love supports me.
I rest my mind forgiving and
blessing all within my circle of love.
I carry loving peaceful thoughts into my sleep.

I fully and freely forgive.

76

Family

I know the laws of my own being and I apply
them to others, especially my family.

I no longer worry as
I try to solve the problems of
my friends and family.

They are not my problems and
I leave their problems alone.

They are not my decisions and
I leave their decisions alone.

They must live their lives and
I leave their lives alone.
I gladly accept my responsibilities and
release those obligations that do not belong to me.

77

I Learn

I learn from
my mis-steps and mis-takes.

I forgive myself.
I don't repeat the same mis-takes.

I no longer idealize the past.
I release the past where the days are a
mirage, gone forever.

I release all resentment and rage.
I release all stress and strain.

Nothing that happened yesterday or
yesteryear can harm or hurt me.

I am blessed with the goodness of life.
I am blessed with the fortune of love.
I am bathed in the Spirit of God.
I enjoy the experience of living today and welcome
the illusionary future with what will be.

78

I Release

I release all negative experiences
of the past and present.
I bless all those connected with painful
memories and believe that only good
shall fill their lives.
I know that just as surely as
God blesses them, He blesses me.
I take the lessons of life from those experiences
and move on with hope,
love, and faith.
I welcome new circumstances that are
right for me as I fulfill the
purpose of my life.
I believe.
I act.
I persist.

79

I Erase

I erase the two devils of the
emotional kingdom—anger and fear—
from my mind.

I release anger's burning passion.
I unlock fear's freezing paralysis.

80

I Spread My Wings

I wandered in the valley of confusion surrounded by
mountains of fear covered with trees of despair.
I sat in a river of tears drowning under waves of sorrow.
Then a flash-flood washed away everything, forcing me to seek a
new way.
The storm is over. I am ready to stop raging against myself.

I am ready to build bridges that cross the whirlpool of envy;
the rapids of tears; the storm of anger; the hurricane of defeat;
the hail of loneliness, the tornado of despair; the blizzard of hate;
the rain of fear; the flood of violence; the tempest of rage;
the lightning flash of sorrow.
The storm is over. I spread my wings.

I seek the silence of solitary spaces;
rushing valley streams to complete my dreams;
towering mountain peaks echoing what God speaks;
waves pounding on the shore promising more and more;
city gardens soaked in rain give me silence once again.
The storm is over. I spread my wings.

I am ready to accept who and what I am. I live each day of my life.
I face every disadvantage with wisdom and faith.
I no longer act like a butterfly pinned painfully to a page.

I unite the fragments of my life. I am certain that no matter what happens,
I can face it, learn from it, and deal with it.
The storm is over. I spread my wings.

I am ready to be responsible for my life and remove barriers that I placed
between God and myself. I allow the Divine to live within me. I praise the good
in my life. I am ready for greatness. I accept new opportunities for prosperity,
love, harmony, and wholeness. Blessings, beyond whatever I can think, feel, taste,
and dream, are ready for me. Life waits for me to act.
The storm is over. I spread my wings.

I dance in the valley of love surrounded by
mountains of dreams covered with trees of faith.
I sit in a river of hope flowing with waves of promise.
A rainbow appears and shows me a new direction.
The storm is over. I fly.

81
I Release Fear

I release fear

I create order
I accept ideas
I learn new ways
I listen
I welcome the unknown
I solve problems
I conquer disappointments
I love

82
I Let Go

I let go of wanting things my way.
I learn patience when
things happen slowly.
I take time to meditate and
calmly review my life.

83

I Am Confident

Inside of me is a place of confidence,
security, and peace where everything is known,
understood, and accepted.

I am a part
of the Universal God who created me and
responds to me as I have faith and belief.
Every problem has an answer and the Magnificent One has all
the answers that come when I need them.
I do not struggle or worry about anything.
I release all obstacles and accept only good, understanding that
whatever I need is supplied.

I accept the Power to heal, to bless, to uplift, and
to inspire.

I Open Myself
to the Circle of Opportunity
and Prosperity
that is endless in the universe.

84 Money

Money is one symbol
of God's gifts.
I recognize my assets and abilities
to reap as I sow money.

The flow of wealth
into my life is plentiful as
the sands on the beaches of the world.

My hands are open as I give from my bank of wealth
while I receive all the money I desire.

The law of circulation is normal and natural for me,
and wealth flows to me as easily as
waves flow in the ocean.

85 Prosperity

I am a magnet for the blessings
of God. My mind has a clear picture of the
prosperity that is mine to claim.

It flows to me freely
and generously from the Infinite Source.
I accept help, guidance, and inspiration to
use the power that is in me.
I recognize the opportunities that exist.
I create a plan for them.
I act.

86

Fruit in My Life

The Wonderful Counselor of Life doesn't
rely on luck or chance
to manifest fruit in my life.

Each person and situation I encounter
are seeds of opportunity for
greater prosperity.

I make good choices in my investments that increase
my bank account and my ability to serve.

87

Money Is Spiritual Substance

I have all the money I desire
with enough to share.
Money is spiritual substance and there is
no shortage of it.

Money and spirit are endless and everlasting.
Through my faith, the Infinite One can produce
one dollar for me as easily as He can produce one
million dollars.
My belief determines what I receive and give.

I express my creativity and become a magnet for money.
It flows to me freely and generously from the Infinite Source.
My mind has a clear picture of the prosperity that is
mine to claim.
I picture everything that I need to live spiritually, abundantly, and lovingly.
My belief determines what I receive and what I give.

Law of Circulation

I practice the law of giving and receiving.
I breathe air without cost,
just as I walk in sunlight without charge.

Money is available to me,
therefore, I receive and give money.
Money is good and with money I can do more to
fulfill my purpose.

I have the right to money and
money is right for me.

I use what I already possess to get the desires of my
heart.
I develop my talents and gifts to generate ideas for
greater prosperity and joy in my life.

89
I Center Myself

I center myself and
release my desire for unnecessary things.

I remove myself from the
insane cravings of the world that
build a wall of debt around me.

I no longer allow advertisements
to dictate how I spend my money.

I don't hoard.
I don't overspend.
I don't steal.

I am a wise
steward of God's riches.

90

God's Gifts

I appreciate the beauty in God's gifts.
I stop and admire the splendor of the flowers.
I am thankful for the water flowing to the ocean.
I am awed by the majesty of the mountains and
the clouds that circle the earth.

As I travel up life's star-case, I thank God for the sunrise
and the dark night lit by the floating moon.
I appreciate the King of Kings whose wisdom operates
the universe in an orderly way,
and I shall do nothing to destroy or harm it.

91

I Am Persistent

I am persistent.
I accept failure as a stepping stone.
Artificial lights created by failures surround me.

Edison tried 6000 times before he found the
formula to create light.
I persist until I find the right material to achieve my goal.
My persistence guarantees I will find the light.

92

I Find Opportunities

I find opportunities where I am today.

It is no accident
that I am in this place
at this time.
I am here to fill a place that no other person can fill.

I seek possibilities, opportunities,
and obligations through relationships
that provide lessons in truth.

93

I Choose

I choose the life more abundant.
The more I have, the more I give;
the more I can experience.
My total being is infused with Divine Energy and
I open my thoughts, feelings, and behaviors
to the larger, the greater, the better.
All my actions are secure and successful as I grow
with the expanding universe.

94

I Am a Mirror

I look into a mirror and
see the truth of the
universe revealed in my spirit.

As day follows night with the sunrise,
I rise to
greet everyone I meet with love,
acceptance, and faith.

I am truly blessed
as the ocean is blessed with water.
My blessings overflow
like flood water.

I Speak Words that are Sweet to the Soul and Healing to the Bones.

95

I Heal My Mind

I need
healing, and
all healing comes from the
Spirit of God within me.

I must heal my mind.
Then I can heal my body.

96

I Laugh

I laugh,
releasing all
tension, frustration, and discouragement.

I take life lightly
and I take myself lightly
as the healing power of laughter
releases my inner light
and all limitations.

97

I Relax

I learn to relax.
From the top of my head to the toes on my feet,
I relax.

I close my eyes and float to a cloud.
I loosen my jaw as the
muscles of my face are free.

My shoulders hang limply and relax.
My arms hang free.
My fingers dangle carelessly.
My stomach is relaxed
as I inhale and exhale from it.

My knees unlock as my legs and feet relax.
I relax my entire body;
every organ,
every tissue,
every nerve,
every muscle.

98

I Begin to Heal

I begin to heal
the ruptures of my heart recovering from
the hurts and disappointments of old loves.

I allow the magic fingers
of time to fade those experiences of
my youth
my innocence
my curiosity
my loneliness
my sexuality
my foolishness.
I accept responsibility for the love I gave
and no longer blame others
who could not love me in
the way I wanted to be loved.
I listen for the gift of love in every
word, touch, and action.
I recognize God expressing love in my life now.

99

I Love My Body

I love my body.
I love the way it functions perfectly.
I think good thoughts about my body.
I see life's beauty in me. I am grateful for my good health.

100

I Rest My Soul

I rest my soul reflecting
on the past.

I analyze my choices and life's changes.
I think about the future and
the growth I desire
in my work
in my relationships
in my body
in my mind.

I reflect on my inner growth,
believing the Lord God knows me and loves me.
I am as precious to Him as anyone who ever lived.
I rest my soul believing
He continually inspires and guides me up the
Ladder of Life.

www.ingramcontent.com/pod-product-compliance
Lightning Source LLC
Chambersburg PA
CBHW070510090426
42735CB00012B/2722